MARRIAGE WITH A NON-MUSLIM
Islamic Perspective in the Light of the Qur'an and Sunnah

Marriage with a Non-Muslim

*Islamic Perspective in the
Light of the Qur'an and Sunnah*

Abdul Quayyum
Ziaul Huq Qutubuddin

Second Edition Published by
Abdul Quayyum (Salmanquayyum@gmail.com)
Ziaul Huq Qutubuddin (zqutub@gmail.com)

First Edition Printed by
Oshi Enterprise
27 Babupara

. Nilkhet, Dhaka 1205, Bangladesh

Contents

1. Introduction

It is not uncommon these days to find Muslim men marrying non-Muslim woman, particularly in the west. Also, while rare, Muslim women are also marrying non-Muslim men.

The objective of this short book is to look at the Qur'an, Ḥadīths and Islamic ruling on this subject and provide an understanding of what is acceptable and what is prohibited in marriage from Islamic perspective. The book has been organized into the following sections:

- Islamic Position on Marriage.

- Understanding *Shirk.*

- Understanding the Terminology *"Mushrik"*, "People of the Book", and "Muslim": This understanding is critical especially in light of how the Qur'anic verses and Aḥadīth which relate to permissibility and prohibition of marriage in Islam.

- Qur'anic Verses on Marriage.

- Aḥadīth on Marriage.

- Related Qur'anic Verses that have Implications on Marriage.

- Related Aḥadīth that have Implications on Marriage.

- Analysis on the Concept of Muslim Marrying *Mushrik.*

- Analysis on the Concept of Muslim Men Marrying Women from the People of the Book.

- Analysis on the Concept of Muslim Women Marrying Men from the People of the Book.

2. Islamic Position on Marriage

The Qur'an stresses upon the people to marry as it is the most effective means to multiply and whereby one can lead a virtuous life free from immorality and emotional inhibition. The following verses from the Qur'an are pertinent to this issue:

And among His Signs is this that He created for you mates from among yourselves that ye may dwell in tranquility with them and He has put love and mercy between your (hearts); verily in that are Signs for those who reflect. (Qur'an Ar-Rum 30:21). Note that all references of Quran verses in this book are from: Quran translation by Yusuf Ali: http://www.islam101.com/quran/yusufAli/

Permitted to you on the night of the fasts is the approach to your wives. They are your garments. And ye are their garments. Allah knoweth what ye used to do secretly among yourselves; but He turned to you and forgave you; so now associate with them and seek what Allah hath ordained for you and eat and drink until the white thread of dawn appear to you distinct from its black thread; then complete your fast till the night appears; but do not associate with your wives while ye are in retreat in the mosques. Those are limits (set by) Allah; approach not nigh thereto. Thus doth Allah make clear His signs to men that they may learn self-restraint. (Qur'an Al-Baqarah 2:187)

It is He who created you from a single person and made his mate of like nature in order that he might dwell with her (in love). When they are united she bears a light burden and carries it about (unnoticed). When she grows heavy they both pray to Allah their Lord (saying): "if Thou givest us a goodly child we vow we shall (ever) be grateful". (Qur'an Al-A'raf 7:189)

The Prophet ﷺ *sunnah* was also to marry. He married a number of times during his lifetime. The Prophet ﷺ said:

When a man has married, he has indeed made his religion half perfect. Then let him fear Allah for the remaining half.

[Reported in Baihaqi and as documented in *The Fundamental Teachings of Qur'an and Ḥadīth* by Nisar Ahmed].

In general, Islam does not approve celibacy and the Prophet ﷺ forbade Uthman ibn Muzun to live a life of celibacy as has been reported in the Ṣaḥīḥ Muslim ḥadīth 3238, and 3239 in volume 2.

However, marriage is only recommended for person who can afford it. According to Ṣaḥīḥ Muslim ḥadīth 3233, volume 2, Abdullah ibn Masud) reported that Allah's Messenger ﷺ said to us:

O young men, those among you who can support a wife should marry, for it restrains eyes (from casting evil glances) and preserves one from immorality; but he who cannot afford it should observe fast, for it is means of controlling the sexual desire.

The Qur'an and Ḥadīth lay down the principle and the basis of marriage and who one can marry.

3. Understanding Shirk

There are many verses in Qur'an that deal with *Shirk*. Similarly there are many Aḥadīths on *Shirk*. The topic of *Shirk* is huge and by itself can be a book. For the purpose of this article only a few verses from the Qur'an, which relate to our article, have been included.

A. Setting up Rival Partner or Invoking others beside Allah. This Includes Trinity.

"................Then do not set up rivals unto Allah (in worship) while you know." (Qur'an Al-Baqarah 2:22)

"Verily, whosoever sets up partners in worship with Allah, then Allah has forbidden Paradise for him, and the Fire will be his abode." (Qur'an An-Nisa' 5:72)

"They do blaspheme who say: Allah is one of three in a Trinity: for there is no god except One Allah. If they desist not from their word (of blasphemy), verily a grievous penalty will befall the blasphemers among them." (Qur'an An-Nisa' 5:73)

"O [my] two companions of prison, are separate lords better or Allah, the One, the Prevailing?" (Qur'an Yusuf 12:39)

"Surely Allah does not forgive that anything should be associated with Him, and forgives what is besides that to whomsoever He pleases, and whoever associates anything with Allah, he devises indeed a great sin." (Qur'an An-Nisa' 4:48)

"Say: "Do ye see what it is ye invoke besides Allah. Show me what it is they have created on earth, or have they a share in the heavens bring me a book (revealed) before this, or any remnant of knowledge (ye may have), if ye are telling the truth!" (Qur'an Al-Ahqaf 46:4)

"Say: 'O People of the Book! come to common terms as between us and you: That we worship none but Allah; that we associate no partners with him; that we erect not, from among ourselves, Lords and patrons other than Allah.' If then they turn back, say ye: 'Bear witness that we (at least) are Muslims (bowing to Allah's Will)'." (Qur'an Ali Imran 3:64)

B. Taking Scholars, Monks, Rabbi as Lord Besides Allah — Who Counters Allah's Commands

"They have taken their scholars and monks as lords besides Allah, and [also] the Messiah, the son of Mary." (Qur'an At-Tawba 9:31).

"All food was lawful to the Children of Israel, except what Israel Made unlawful for itself, before the Law (of Moses) was revealed. Say: 'Bring ye the Law and study it, if ye be men of truth'." (Qur'an Ali Imran 3:93)

"Say: 'O People of the Book! ye have no ground to stand upon unless ye stand fast by the Law, the Gospel, and all

the revelation that has come to you from your Lord.' It is the revelation that cometh to thee from thy Lord, that increaseth in most of them their obstinate rebellion and blasphemy. But sorrow thou not over (these) people without Faith." (Qur'an Al-Ma'ida 5:68)

"No just estimate of Allah do they make when they say: 'Nothing doth Allah send down to man (by way of revelation)' Say: 'Who then sent down the Book which Moses brought?- a light and guidance to man: But ye make it into (separate) sheets for show, while ye conceal much (of its contents): therein were ye taught that which ye knew not- neither ye nor your fathers.' Say: '(Allah) (sent it down)': Then leave them to plunge in vain discourse and trifling." (Qur'an Al-An'am 6:91)

C. Taking Uzair and Jesus as the son of God

"The Jews call 'Uzair a son of Allah, and the Christians call Christ the son of Allah. That is a saying from their mouth; (in this) they but imitate what the unbelievers of old used to say. Allah's curse be on them: how they are deluded away from the Truth!" (Qur'an At-Tawba 9:30)

"They take their priests and their anchorites to be their lords in derogation of Allah, and (they take as their Lord) Christ the son of Mary; yet they were commanded to worship but One Allah: there is no god but He. Praise and glory to Him: (Far is He) from having the partners they associate (with Him)." (Qur'an At-Tawba 9:31)

D. Worshipping Idols as God

"They said: 'We worship idols, and we remain constantly in attendance on them'." (Qur'an Ash-Shu'ara 26:71)

"For ye do worship idols besides Allah, and ye invent falsehood. The things that ye worship besides Allah have no power to give you sustenance: then seek ye sustenance from Allah, serve Him, and be grateful to Him: to Him will be your return." (Qur'an Al-Ankabut 29:17)

"Will ye call upon Baal and forsake the Best of Creators." (Qur'an As-Saffat 37:125)

E. Worshipping Sun as God

"I found her and her people worshipping the sun besides Allah: Satan has made their deeds seem pleasing in their eyes, and has kept them away from the Path,- so they receive no guidance." (Qur'an An-Naml 27:24)

F. Worshipping Men as God

"(Pharaoh) said: 'If thou dost put forward any god other than me, I will certainly put thee in prison!'" (Qur'an Ash-Shu'ara 26:29)

4. Understanding the Terminology "Mushrik", "Muslim" and "People of the Book"

Understanding the above terminology is critical for the rest of the article. It provides the basis and the meat for subsequent analysis The Qur'an has labeled or provided names to many a nation that has passed away as an identifying factor, *e.g.*, the Nation of Ad, the Nation of Thamud, the Nation of Lut, and Firaun (Pharoah). Accordingly, it is not surprising that Allah has identified the idolaters of Mecca as "*Mushrik*" or the followers of Prophet Ibrahim who were provided the Holy book from Allah as "People of the Book", or Muslims who submitted to Allah and accepted Islam.

The rest of this section focuses on understanding what each of these term means; which nation or people falls into these categories; what is their religion and how do their worship relate to Allah and s*hirk*.

A. Understanding the Term "Mushrik"

A *Mushrik* is one who commits *Shirk*. Normally the term *Mushrik* refers to the idol worshippers. However, anyone who performs the following, as discussed in detail in Section III "Understanding *Shirk*", irrespective of the fact that he calls himself Muslim or from People of the Book, commits *Shirk* and is called a *Mushrik*.

- Setting Rival/Partner or Invoking other beside Allah— This includes those who believe in Trinity.

- Taking Scholars, Monks, Rabbi as Lord beside Allah—*i.e.*, those who Counters Allah's Commands.

- Taking Uzair (*Alaihes-Salam*) and Jesus/Isa (*Alaihes-Salam*) as the sons of God.

- Worshipping Idols, Men or Sun as God.

B. Understanding the Term "Muslim"

A Muslim is one who accepts whole-heartedly the fact that Allah is one and that Muhammad is His messenger, along with the elements of *Aqida* (*e.g.* believing in Allah, Allah's Prophets/ Messengers, His, Books, His angels, the last Day (Day of Judgement), *Qadar* (pre- destination or Divine Will) and life after death). Muslims, as with all other religions will be judged by Allah. Based on their actions (coupled with the Mercy of Allah), a Muslim/Muslima can either go to heaven or to hell and, if in hell, will (eventually) return to heaven.

C. Understanding the Term People of the Book

This term relates specifically to the nations of Jews and Christians who were descendents of Prophet Ibrahim and to whom the Holy Scriptures of Torah (to Jews) and Injīl (to Christians) were revealed by the Al-mighty Allah.

The Qur'an separates the People of the Book into two Categories:

1. Believers and.

2. Non-Believers (Kafir or Mushrik).

As described in the following two Qur'anic verses:

"It is He who has created you; and of you are some that are Unbelievers, and some that are Believers: and Allah sees well all that ye do." (Qur'an At-Taghabun 64:2)

"Ye are the best of peoples, evolved for mankind, enjoining what is right, forbidding what is wrong, and believing in Allah. If only the People of the Book had faith, it were best for them: among them are some who have faith, but most of them are perverted transgressors." (Qur'an Ali Imran 3:110)

1. The Believers from the People of the Book

Following are some of the verses related to Believers from the People of the Book.

"And when it is recited to them, they say: 'We believe therein, for it is the Truth from our Lord: indeed we have been Muslims (bowing to Allah's Will) from before this'." (Qur'an Al-Qasas 28:53)

"Not all of them are alike. Of the People of the book are a portion that stands (for the right); they rehearse the signs of Allah all night long and then prostrates themselves in adoration." (Qur'an Ali Imran 3:113)

"They believe in Allah and the Last Day; they enjoin what is right and forbid what is wrong; and they (hasten in emulation) in (all) good works; they are in the ranks of the righteous." (Qur'an Ali Imran 3:114)

"Of the good that they do nothing will be rejected of them; for Allah knoweth well those that do right." (Qur'an Ali Imran 3:115)

"Among the People of the Book are some who if entrusted with a hoard of gold will (readily) pay it back; others who

if entrusted with a single silver coin will not repay it unless thou constantly stood demanding because they say 'There is no call on us (to keep faith) with these ignorant (pagans).' But they tell a lie against Allah and (well) they know it." (Qur'an Ali Imran 3:75)

"Nay. Those that keep their plighted faith and act aright verily Allah loves those who act aright." (Qur'an Ali Imran 3:76)

"If only they had stood fast by the Law, the Gospel and all the revelation that was sent to them from their Lord they would have enjoyed happiness from every side. There is from among them a party on the right course; but many of them follow a course that is evil." (Qur'an Al-Ma'ida 5:66)

"They believe in Allah and the Last Day; they enjoin what is right and forbid what is wrong; and they hasten (in emulation) in (all) good works: They are in the ranks of the righteous." (Qur'an Al-Ma'ida 3:114)

"What cause can we have not to believe in Allah and the truth which has come to us, seeing that we long for our Lord to admit us to the company of the righteous?" (Qur'an Al-Ma'ida 5:84)

"And for this their prayer hath Allah rewarded them with gardens, with rivers flowing underneath, —their eternal home. Such is the recompense of those who do good." (Qur'an Al-Ma'ida 5:85)

While the believers from the People of the Book are clear from the above verses, the Qur'an summarizes the believers in the following verse:

"And there are, certainly, among the People of the Book, those who believe in Allah, in the revelation to you, and in the revelation to them, bowing in humility to Allah. They will not sell the Signs of Allah for a miserable gain! For

them is a reward with their Lord, and Allah is swift in account." (Qur'an Ali Imran 3:199)

An example of such a person is Waraqa Ibn Nawfal, cousin of Hazrat Khadija and wife of the Prophet ﷺ. Waraqa immediately believed in the revelation of the Qur'an sent to Prophet Muhammad ﷺ when he was first informed.

The present-day Christians and Jews who follow their religions and are aware of Prophet Muhammad ﷺ and the message of Islam and have not accepted them, are certainly not believers based on the above Qur'an verse and also the Prophet's Ḥadīth as reported on the authority of Abu Huraira that the Messenger of Allah ﷺ observed:

> "By Him in whose hand is the life of Muhammad, he who amongst the community of Jews and Christians hears about me, but does not affirm his belief in that which I have been sent with and dies in that state (of disbelief), he shall be but one of the denizens of Hell-Fire"

[Muslim Ḥadīth 284 in Volume 1]

However, if we find any Christians or Jews following their original scriptures and believing in the Oneness of Allah without committing any type of Shirk, as discussed earlier, and who have never heard of Islam or Prophet Muhammad's ρ message, these people can be described as *Ahlul Fitra* or Believers. Invitation to Islam should be provided, and if they accept Islam then they continue to be true Believers. If they reject, then they become Disbelievers and subject to Allah's punishment as described above.

2. The Non-Believers from the People of the Book

The non-believers from the People of the Book can be categorized as either: People of the Book who are *Mushrik* or People of the Book who are Disbelievers (*Kafirs*)

i.   People of the Book who are Mushrik

The Qur'an is very clear that the majority of the people of the book are Mushrik. The following verses attest to this conclusion:

"In blasphemy indeed are those that say that Allah is Christ the son of Mary. Say: 'Who then hath the least power against Allah if His Will were to destroy Christ the son of Mary his mother and all everyone that is on the earth? For to Allah belongeth the dominion of the heavens and the earth and all that is between. He createth what He pleaseth. For Allah hath power over all things'." (Qur'an Al-Ma'ida 5:17)

"They say: 'Become Jews or Christians if ye would be guided (To salvation).' Say thou: 'Nay! (I would rather) the Religion of Abraham the True, and he joined not gods with Allah'." (Qur'an Al-Baqarah 2:135)

"Abraham was not a Jew nor yet a Christian; but he was true in Faith, and bowed his will to Allah's (Which is Islam), and he joined not gods with Allah." (Qur'an Ali Imran 3:67)

"They do blaspheme who say: '(Allah) is Christ the son of Mary.' But said Christ: 'O Children of Israel! Worship Allah, my Lord and your Lord.' Whoever joins other gods with Allah, Allah will forbid him the garden, and the Fire will be his abode. There will for the wrong-doers be no one to help." (Qur'an Al-Ma'ida 5:72)

"They do blaspheme who say: Allah is one of three in a Trinity: for there is no god except One Allah. If they desist not from their word (of blasphemy), verily a grievous penalty will befall the blasphemers among them." (Qur'an Al-Ma'ida 5:73)

"Those who reject (Truth) among the People of the Book and among the Polytheists will be in hell-fire to dwell therein (for aye). They are the worst of creatures." (Qur'an Al-Bayyina 98:6)

"The Jews call 'Uzair a son of Allah and the Christians call Christ the son of Allah. That is a saying from their mouth; (in this) they but imitate what the unbelievers of old used to say. Allah's curse be on them: how they are deluded away from the Truth!" (Qur'an At-Tawba 9:30)

"They take their priests and their anchorites to be their lords in derogation of Allah, and (they take as their Lord) Christ the son of Mary; yet they were commanded to worship but One Allah: there is no god but He. Praise and glory to Him: (Far is He) from having the partners they associate (with Him)." (Qur'an At-Tawba 9:31)

"Say: 'O People of the Book! come to common terms as between us and you: That we worship none but Allah; that we associate no partners with him; that we erect not, from among ourselves, Lords and patrons other than Allah.' If then they turn back, say ye: 'Bear witness that we (at least) are Muslims (bowing to Allah's Will)'." (Qur'an Ali Imran 3:64)

The *Aḥadīth of the Prophet* provides similar position on People of the Book being *Mushriks*. Below are examples of few Aḥadīth.

Abu Sa'id al-Khudri reported: Some people during the lifetime of the Messenger of Allah ﷺ said: Messenger of Allah! shall we see our Lord on the Day of Resurrection? The Messenger of Allah ρ said: Yes, ... When the Day of Resurrection comes, a *Mu'adhdhin* (a proclaimer) would proclaim: Let every people follow what they used to worship. Then all who worshipped idols and stones besides Allah would fall into the Fire, till only the righteous and the vicious and some of the people of the book who worshipped Allah are left. Then the Jews would be summoned, and it would be said to them: What did you worship? They will say: We worshipped 'Uzair, son of Allah. It would be said to them: You tell a lie; Allah had never had a spouse or a son. What do you want now? They would say: We feel thirsty, O our Lord! Quench our thirst. They would be directed (to a certain direction) and asked: Why don't you go there to drink water? Then they would be pushed towards the Fire (and they would find to their great dismay that) it was but a mirage (and the raging flames of fire) would be consuming one another, and they would fall into the Fire. Then the Christians would be summoned, and it would be said to them: What did you worship? They would say: We worshipped Jesus, son of Allah. It would be said to them: You tell a lie; Allah did not take for Himself either a spouse or a son. Then it would be said to them: What do you want? They would say: Thirsty we are, O our Lord! Quench our thirst. They would be directed (to a certain direction) and asked: Why don't you go there to get water? But they would be pushed and gathered together towards the Hell, which was like a mirage to them, and the flames would consume one another. They would fall Into the Fire, till no one is left except he who worshipped Allah, be he pious or sinful. The Lord of the Universe, Glorified and Exalted, would come to them in a form recognizable to them and say; What are you looking for? Every people follow that which they worshipped ...

[Muslim Ḥadīth 0352 in Book 1]

Abu 'Ubaydah bin al-Jarrah narrated: The last words spoken by the Prophet ﷺ were: "Expel the Jews of Hijaz and the people of Najran (*i.e.* Christians) from the Arabian Peninsula. And know that the most evil of people are those who take the graves of their prophets as places of worship."

[Musnad Ahmad, Ḥadīth 1691]

In another version of the report the wording is:

Ibn 'Abbas narrated: The Prophet ﷺ on his deathbed, gave three orders, [one of them was] "Expel the polytheists (al-*mushrikin*) from the Arabian Peninsula."

[Ṣaḥīḥ Bukhari, Hadith 3053.

In relation to the above Ḥadīth, Al-Albani (d. 1420/2000) commented to Bukhari's version saying:

"In this is the evidence for usage of the word "*mushrik*" for People of the Book, for they are intended in this report (using the word "*mushrikin*") as evidenced by the ḥadīth prior to it (*i.e.* report of Abu 'Ubaydah)."

[Al-Albani, Silsala al-Ahadith as-Sahiha, Vol.3, 125]
Source: http://thedefiance.co/marriage_with_disbelievers

The above *Qur'anic Ayats and Aḥadīth* on the People of the Book can be best summarized as follows:

- Christians who ascribe Jesus as the son of God commits *Shirk.*
- Christians who ascribe to the concept of Trinity or ascribe Jesus as God commits *Shirk.*
- Jews who ascribe Uzair as the son of God commits *Shirk.*
- Christians and Jews who take their Scholars, Rabbis and Monks as God, beside Allah, in ordaining right and wrong commits *Shirk.*

The status of Jews who potentially believe in Torah, and potentially believe in the Oneness of God but reject Islam and also present-day Christians who claim to believe in the Oneness of God (Unitarianism) but reject Islam will be discussed below under People of the Book who are Disbelievers.

ii.   People of the Book who are Disbelievers

Two group of people, as listed below, will be discussed, and analyzed to see if they are really disbelievers (Kafirs) or should be categorized as Mushrik

a. Jews who Potentially Believe in Torah and Potentially in the Oneness of God but Reject Islam:

If we look at the following two verses and infer from it then we could come to the conclusion that every member of the people of the Book are *Mushrik* as opposed to a section of them being disbelievers: a) Qur'an Verse Al-Baqarah 2:135:

"They say: 'Become Jews or Christians if ye would be guided (To salvation).' Say thou: 'Nay! (I would rather) the Religion of Abraham the True, and he joined not gods with Allah'."

And Qur'anic Verse Ali Imran 3:67:

"Abraham was not a Jew nor yet a Christian; but he was true in Faith, and bowed his will to Allah's (Which is Islam), and he joined not gods with Allah."

Based on the above Qur'anic verses and discussions in earlier sections labeled as "The Believers from the People of the Book" and "People of the Book who are *Mushrik*", the conclusion is that the People of the Book are either believers or *Mushrik*.

Similarly, if we look at the Qur'anic verse on *"following own Nafs or passion"*, or taking the Scholars and Rabbis as Lord, this group of people can also be called Mushrik as they have allowed their Scholars and

Rabbis to change the Torah to meet their "*Nafs*", *i.e.,* changing the punishment for adultery for stoning to death to something different, as mentioned in Muslim Ḥadīth 4211 in Volume 3, which reads:

"Abdullah ibn 'Umar reported that a Jew and a Jewess were brought to Allah's Messenger ﷺ who had committed adultery. Allah's Messenger ﷺ came to the Jews and said: What do you find in Torah for one who commits adultery? They said: We darken their faces and make them ride on the donkey with their faces turned to the opposite direction (and their backs touching each other), and then they are taken round (the city). He said: Bring Torah if you are truthful. They brought it and recited it until when they came to the verse pertaining to stoning, the person who was reading placed his hand on the verse pertaining to stoning and read (only that which was) between his hands and what was subsequent to that. Abdullah ibn Salim who was at that time with the Messenger of Allah ﷺ said: Command him (the reciter) to lift his hand. He lifted it and there was, underneath that, the verse pertaining to stoning. Allah's Messenger ﷺ pronounced judgment about both of them and they were stoned. Abdullah b. 'Umar said: I was one of those who stoned them, and I saw him (the Jew) protecting her (the Jewess) with his body."

The Qur'an is also explicit about the Jews hiding verses in the Torah as shown by the following:

"*O people of the Scripture (Jews and Christians)! Now has come to you Our Messenger (Muhammad) explaining to you much of that which you used to hide from the Scripture and pass over (i.e. leaving out without explaining) much. Indeed, there has*

come to you from Allah a light and a plain Book."
(Qur'an Al-Ma'ida 5:15)

And also, Qur'an verse Ali Imran 3:187:

"(And remember) when Allah took a covenant from those who were given the Scripture (Jews and Christians) to make it known and clear to mankind, and not to hide it, but they threw it away behind their backs, and purchased with it some miserable gain! And indeed worst is that which they bought."

Also, the opinion of the *Sahabas* (Hazrat Ibn Abbas and Ibn Umar), when the marriage verse Al-Baqarah 2:221 was revealed was that the word "*Mushrikun* included People of the Book".

In summary, based on the Qur'anic and Aḥadīth discussion above, all Jews can be categorized as *Mushrik*. However, for analysis purpose, we will assume that a portion of the Jews (who exist now or possibly in the future and who does not commit *Shirk*) can be categorized as simply disbelievers (*Kafirs*) or deviant as described in Sūrah Fatihah—those who know and reject Islam. Also, included in this category are the people who never got the message of Islam—people who are called *Ahlul Fitra*.

b. Christians who Potentially Believe in Bible and Potentially in the Oneness of God but Reject Islam:

This section relates to followers of Unitarianism in Christianity. Information on this section is based on an article on Unitarianism and found on the Web at: http://carm.org/what-unitarianism

Unitarianism is the belief that God exists in one person - not three. It is a denial of the doctrine of the Trinity as well as the full divinity of Jesus. Therefore, it is not the same as known Christianity. There are several groups that fall under this umbrella: Jehovah's Witnesses, Christadelphianism, The Way International, *etc.* Additional beliefs generally held by Unitarian Universalists are:

- Salvation is by grace through faith and not by works in any way.

- Jesus became the Son of God at His baptism.

- The Holy Spirit is not a person, does not have a will, *etc.*

- There now is and will be rewards and punishments according to one's actions, but this does not consist of the traditional doctrine of hell.

- Human reason and experience should be the final authority in determining spiritual truth.

Instead of God and his word being the final authority on truth and error or right and wrong, Unitarian Universalists subject God and His word to their understanding, feeling, and reason.

Below is another view on Unitarianism. This reflects information From Wikipedia, the free encyclopedia.

Unitarianism is a Christian theological movement named for its understanding of God as one person, in direct contrast to Trinitarianism, which defines God as three persons coexisting consubstantially in one being. Unitarians maintain that Jesus is in some sense the "son" of God but that he is not the one God. Unitarianism is also known for the rejection of several other conventional Christian doctrines, including the doctrines of original sin, predestination, and, in more recent history, biblical inerrancy (that the Bible is without error or fault in all its teaching)

Unitarians have liberal views of God, Jesus, the world and purpose of life as revealed through reason, scholarship, science, philosophy, scripture and other prophets and religions. They believe that reason and belief are complementary, and that religion and science can co-exist and guide them in their understanding of nature and God. They also do not enforce belief in creeds or dogmatic or formulas. Although there is flexibility in the nuances of belief or basic truth for the individual Unitarian Christian, general principles of faith have been recognized as a way to bind the group in some commonality. Adherents generally accept religious pluralism and find value in all teachings but remain committed to their core belief in Christ's teachings. Unitarians generally value a secular society in which government is kept separate from religious affairs. Most contemporary Unitarian Christians believe that one's personal moral convictions guide one's political activities, and that a secular society is the most viable, just and fair. Unitarian Christians reject the doctrine of some Christian denominations that God chooses to redeem or save only those certain individuals that accept the creeds of, or affiliate with, a specific church or religion, from a common ruin or corruption of the mass of humanity.

In summary, based on the above discussion, one can easily see that the followers of Unitarianism are *Mushriks*. They believe in Jesus being the son of God, and they do not follow the standard Bible or Torah but have come up with their own definition and understanding of religion. In short, they are "following their own *Nafs* or Passions" and have defined a religion that conforms to their liking and desires where they regard Jesus as the son of God —and hence they are committing *Shirk* and are *Mushrik*. However, for analysis purpose, we will assume that a portion of the Unitarian or people of Christian faith (who exist now or possibly in the future and who does not commit *Shirk*) can be categorized as simply disbelievers (*Kafirs*) or deviant as described in Sūrah Fatihah—those who know and reject Islam. Also, included in this category are the people who never got the message of Islam—people who are called *Ahlul Fitra*.

5. *Qur'anic Verses on Marriage*

The relevant verses from the Qur'an on marriage are below:

The verse: *"Do not marry unbelieving women (idolaters) until they believe; a slave woman who believes is better than an unbelieving woman even though she allure you. Nor marry (your girls) to unbelievers until they believe: a man slave who believes is better than an unbeliever even though he allure you. Unbelievers do (but) beckon you to the fire. But Allah beckons by His grace to the Garden (of Bliss) and forgiveness and makes His Signs clear to mankind: that they may celebrate His praise".* (Qur'an Al-Baqarah 2:221)

Comments: This is the main verse which forbids marriage to a *Mushrik*—one who commits *Shirk,* as discussed earlier in Section III "Understanding *Shirk*" and Section IV "Understanding the Terminology *Mushrik,* Muslim and People of the Book". This is a verse that was revealed in Madinah as part of a whole series of other verses which laid down religious, social and economic rules for the people to follow irrespective of their ethnicity. According to Tafsir Ibn Kathir Volume 3, page 104, Ibn Abi Hatim recorded that Abu Malik

Al-Ghifari said that Ibn Abbas said that when this *Ayat* was revealed, the people did not marry the pagan women. When the verse *"lawful to you in marriage are chaste women from the People of the believers and chaste women from the People of the Scriptures before your time"*, was revealed, they married women from the People of the Book. In the same Tafsir of Ibn Kathir and reported by Bukhari, Ibn Umar said *"I do not know of a bigger Shirk than her saying that Jesus is her Lord."*

> The verse: *"This day are (all) things good and pure made lawful unto you. The food of the People of the Book is lawful unto you and yours is lawful unto them. (Lawful unto you in marriage) are (not only) chaste women who are believers but chaste women among the People of the Book revealed before your time when ye give them their due dowers and desire chastity not lewdness nor secret intrigues. If anyone rejects faith fruitless is his work and in the Hereafter he will be in the ranks of those who have lost (all spiritual good)"*. (Qur'an Al-Ma'ida 5:5)

Comments: This is the main verse from the Qur'an which permits Muslim man marrying woman of the People of the Book. This is one of the last verses that were revealed. A vast number of scholars believe that this verse is an exception to the verse 2:221 which forbade Muslim men marrying *Mushrik* women. The Scholars believe this verse provides an exception to marry women of the People of the Book. Some *Sahabas* disagree as well as some prominent Imam of the four *Madhhabs.* This will be discussed later.

> The verse: *"The fornicator does not marry except a fornicatress (Female) or an idolatress, and the fornicatress shall not marry anyone but a fornicator or an idolator and that (marrying them) is haram for the believers"*. (Qur'an An-Nur 24:3)

Comments: A believer, either men or women, is forbidden to marry a fornicator. This includes marrying a Muslim fornicator unless he or she repents. A fornicator is not in Islam when he/she is committing act of adultery according to Bukhari Ḥadīth 484 in Volume 7 as narrated by Abu Huraira:

> "The Prophet said, "An adulterer, at the time he is committing illegal sexual intercourse is not a believer; and a person, at the time of drinking an alcoholic drink is not a believer; and a thief, at the time of stealing, is not a believer.""

Ibn Shihab said: 'Abdul Malik bin Abi Bakr bin 'Abdur-Rahman bin Al- Harith bin Hisham told me that Abu Bakr used to narrate that narration to him on the authority of Abu Huraira. He used to add that Abu Bakr used to mention, besides the above cases,

> "And he who robs (takes illegally something by force) while the people are looking at him, is not a believer at the time he is robbing (taking) it".

Accordingly, it can be inferred from this Qur'anic *Ayat* and the Ḥadīth mentioned above that the Muslim woman can only marry a believing Muslim man.

> The Verse: *"Women impure are for men impure, and men impure for women impure and women of purity are for men of purity, and men of purity are for women of purity: these are not affected by what people say: for them there is forgiveness and a provision honorable".* (Qur'an An-Nur 24:26)

Comments: This verse complements the meaning and substance of verse 24:3 discussed above.

The Verse: *"O ye who believe! When there come to you believing women refugees, examine (and test) them: Allah knows best as to their Faith: if ye ascertain that they are Believers, then send them not back to the Unbelievers (Kafirs). They are not lawful (wives) for the Unbelievers, nor are the (Unbelievers) lawful (husbands) for them. But pay the Unbelievers what they have spent (on their dower), and there will be no blame on you if ye marry them on payment of their dower to them. But hold not to the guardianship of unbelieving women: ask for what ye have spent on their dowers, and let the (Unbelievers) ask for what they have spent (on the dowers of women who come over to you). Such is the command of Allah: He judges (with justice) between you. And Allah is Full of Knowledge and Wisdom".* (Qur'an Al-Mumtahina 60:10)

Comments: This is another verse which confirms that Muslim woman cannot marry an unbeliever (*Kafir*), as they are unlawful to them. Imam Ash Shawkani in his *tafsir* book "*Fathul Qadīr*" states that this verse is a strong proof (*Dalīl*) which prohibits believing woman marrying a disbelieving man. Imam Qurtubi also states that this verse is the biggest *Dalīl* which prohibits believing woman marrying a disbelieving man.

6. Aḥadīth on Marriage

Below are some Aḥadīths related to marriage with women from the People of the Book.

Muslim Ḥadīth 3457, volume 2: Abu Huraira reported that Allah's Messenger ﷺ as saying: A woman may be married for four reasons: for her property, her status, her beauty, and her religion. So, try to get one who is religious. May your hand be besmeared with dust. A similar ḥadīth was reported in Muslim Hadith 3458.

Bukhari Ḥadīth 209, Volume 7 and narrated by Nafi: Whenever Ibn 'Umar was asked about marrying a Christian lady or a Jewess, he would say: "Allah has made it unlawful for the believers to marry ladies who ascribe partners in worship to Allah, and I do not know of a greater thing, as regards to ascribing partners in worship, etc. to Allah, than that a lady should say that Jesus is her Lord although he is just one of Allah's slaves."

Bukhari Ḥadīth 387, Vol 7: Abu Thalaba Al-Khusani narrated: I said, "O Allah's Prophet! ﷺ We are living in a land ruled by the people of the Scripture; Can we take our meals in their utensils? In that land there is plenty of game and I hunt the game with my bow and with my hound that is not trained and with my trained hound. Then what is lawful for me to eat?" He said, "As for what you have mentioned about the people of the Scripture, if you can get utensils other than theirs, do not eat out of theirs, but if you cannot get other than theirs, wash their utensils and eat out of it. If you hunt an animal with your bow after mentioning Allah's Name, eat of it. And if you hunt something with your trained hound after mentioning Allah's Name, eat of it, and if you hunt something with your untrained hound (and get it before it dies) and slaughter it, eat of it."

Muslim Ḥadīth 284 in Volume 1: It is reported on the authority of Abu Huraira that the Messenger of Allah (ﷺ) observed: "By Him in whose hand is the life of Muhammad, he who amongst the community of Jews and Christians hears about me, but does not affirm his belief in that which I have been sent with and dies in that state (of disbelief), he shall be but one of the denizens of Hell-Fire".

Sunan of Abu Daud, Ḥadīth 4020 narrated by Ibn Umar, who reported: The Prophet ﷺ said: He who copies any people is one of them.

Ṣaḥīḥ Muslim Ḥadīth 3465, volume 2: Abdullah b. Amr reported Allah's Messenger ﷺ as saying: The whole world is a provision, and the best object of benefit of the world is the pious woman.

Comments: This section highlights the following points:

- One should try to marry one who is religious. Certainly a Muslim woman is more religious than a Christian or Jew, who have been condemned to Hell

- Ibn Umar considers the Christians to be *Mushrik* and accordingly is strongly against Muslim Man marrying them

- Muslims are requested not to follow the people of the book and if they do, then they become like them and have strayed away from the Straight Path. Similarly, Muslims are asked not to eat on the utensils of the people of the book, if they can get other proper utensils.

7. Related Qur'anic Verses that have Implication on Marriage

Verses from Qur'an must be understood in reference to the context of the verse itself and as well as the overall context and message of the Qur'an. Accordingly, I have listed here various verses from the Qur'an which *Ulema / fukaha* (jurists), among other things, consider when making a decision whether a Muslim man can marry a woman of the People of the Book.

"O ye who believe! Take not into your intimacy those outside your ranks: They will not fail to corrupt you. They only desire your ruin: Rank hatred has already appeared from their mouths: What their hearts conceal is far worse. We have made plain to you the Signs, if ye have wisdom." (Qur'an Ali Imran 3:118)

"Let not the believers take for friends or helpers unbelievers rather than believers; if any do that in nothing will there be help from Allah; except by way of precaution that ye may guard yourselves from them. But Allah cautions you (to remember) Himself for the final goal is to Allah." (Qur'an Ali Imran 3:28)

"O ye who believe! Take not the Jews and the Christians for your friends and protectors: They are but friends and protectors to each other. And he amongst you that turns to them (for friendship) is of them. Verily Allah guideth not a people unjust." (Qur'an Al-Ma'ida 5:51)

(*Note*: This verse was actually revealed about the hypocrites, condemning them for taking Jews and Christians as friends with the intention of fighting against the Muslims. The following verse 5:57 clarifies this)

"O ye who believe! Take not for friends and protectors those who take your religion for a mockery or sport,— whether among those who received the Scripture before you, or among those who reject Faith; but fear ye Allah, if ye have faith (indeed)." (Qur'an Al-Ma'ida 5:57)

"Thou seest many of them turning in friendship to the unbelievers. Evil indeed are (the works) which their souls have sent forward before them (with the result) that Allah's wrath is on them and in torment will they abide." (Qur'an Al-Ma'ida 5:80)

"Eat not of (meats) on which Allah's name hath not been pronounced: That would be impiety. But the evil ones ever inspire their friends to contend with you if ye were to obey them, ye would indeed be Pagans." (Qur'an Al-An'am 6:121)

"For the worst of beasts in the sight of Allah are those who reject Him: They will not believe." (Qur'an Al-Anfal 8:55)

"Yea to those who take for friends' unbelievers rather than believers: is it honor they seek among them? Nay all honor is with Allah." (Qur'an An-Nisa' 4:139)

"O you who believe! do not take your fathers and your brothers for guardians if they love unbelief more than belief; and whoever of you takes them for a guardian, these it is that are the unjust." (Qur'an At-Tawba 9:23)

"O ye who believe! take not My enemies and yours as friends (or protectors) offering them (your) love even though they have rejected the Truth that has come to you and have (on the contrary) driven out the Prophet and yourselves (from your homes) (simply) because ye believe in Allah your Lord! If ye have come out to strive in My Way and to seek My Good Pleasure (take them not as friends) holding secret converse of love (and friendship) with them: for I know full well all that ye conceal and all that ye reveal. **And any of you that do this has strayed from the Straight Path.**" (Qur'an Al-Mumtahina 60:1)

"O ye who believe! turn not (for friendship) to people on whom is the Wrath of Allah. Of the Hereafter they are already in despair just as the Unbelievers are in despair about those (buried) in graves." (Qur'an Al-Mumtahina 60:13)

Comments: The above verses can be summarized as follows:

- Don't take the Jews and Christians as your friend (not relevant in matters such as classmates, colleagues, business dealings *etc.*) or protector. In line with the Divine principle ordained in the Qur'an and Sunnah, justice and fairness must be done, and oppressed people should be helped regardless of faith.

- Don't take your fathers and brothers as guardians if they love unbelief (*Kufr*) over belief.

- If you obey the Disbelievers (*Kafirs*) and perform acts that are contrary to Islam, then you become like them.

- If you turn toward them (*Kafir*) in friendship, then you become like them and have strayed away from the Straight Path.

8. Related Aḥadīth that have Implication on Marriage

The following are a collection of Aḥadīth that are relevant to the subject and should be considered while making any decision related to marrying someone from the People of the Book:

Muslim ḥadīth 284 in Volume 1: It is reported on the authority of Abu Huraira that the Messenger of Allah ﷺ observed: "By Him in whose hand is the life of Muhammad, he who amongst the community of Jews and Christians hears about me, but does not affirm his belief in that which I have been sent with and dies in that state (of disbelief), he shall be but one of the denizens of Hell-Fire".

Sunan of Abu Daud, ḥadīth 4020 narrated by Ibn Umar, who reported: The Prophet ﷺ said: "He who copies any people is one of them".

9. Analysis on the Concept of Muslim Marrying Mushrik

There is a unanimous (100%) agreement among the Islamic scholars concerning the prohibition of marrying a *Mushrik* (idolators). The Qur'an is very clear and forbids marrying male or female who are *Mushrik* (idolators) in the following verses:

Quran Verse: "Do not marry unbelieving women (idolaters) until they believe; a slave woman who believes is better than an unbelieving woman even though she allure you. Nor marry (your girls) to unbelievers until they believe: a man slave who believes is better than an unbeliever even though he allure you. Unbelievers do (but) beckon you to the fire. But Allah beckons by His grace to the Garden (of Bliss) and forgiveness and makes His Signs clear to mankind: that they may celebrate His praise". (Qur'an Al-Baqarah 2:221)

Comments: This is the main verse which forbids marriage to a *Mushrik*—one who commits *Shirk*, as discussed earlier in Section III "Understanding *Shirk*" and Section IV

"Understanding the Terminology Mushrik, Muslim and People of the Book". This is a verse that was revealed in Madinah as part of a whole series of other verses which laid down religious, social and economic rules for the people to follow irrespective of their ethnicity. According to Tafsir Ibn Kathir Volume 3, page 104, Ibn Abi Hatim recorded that Abu Malik Al-Ghifari said that Ibn Abbas said that when this *Ayat* was revealed, the people did not marry the pagan women. When the verse "*lawful to you in marriage are chase women from the People of the believers and chaste women from the People of the Scriptures before your time*", was revealed, they married women from the People of the Book. In the same Tafsir of Ibn Kathir and reported by Bukhari, Ibn Umar said "*I do not know of a bigger Shirk than her saying that Jesus is her Lord.*"

Quran Verse: "O ye who believe! When there come to you believing women refugees, examine (and test) them: Allah knows best as to their Faith: if ye ascertain that they are Believers, then send them not back to the Unbelievers. They are not lawful (wives) for the Unbelievers, nor are the (Unbelievers) lawful (husbands) for them. But pay the Unbelievers what they have spent (on their dower), and there will be no blame on you if ye marry them on payment of their dower to them. But hold not to the guardianship of unbelieving women: ask for what ye have spent on their dowers, and let the (Unbelievers) ask for what they have spent (on the dowers of women who come over to you). Such is the command of Allah: He judges (with justice) between you. And Allah is Full of Knowledge and Wisdom." (Qur'an Al-Mumtahina 60:10)

Comments: This is another verse which confirms that Muslim woman cannot marry an unbeliever (*Kafir*), as they are unlawful to them. Imam Ash Shawkani in his *tafsir* book

"*Fathul Qadīr*" states that this verse is a strong proof (*Dalīl*) which prohibits believing woman marrying a disbelieving man. Imam Qurtubi also states that this verse is the biggest *Dalīl* which prohibits believing woman marrying a disbelieving man.

Accordingly, marrying somebody who has committed *Shirk* is prohibited in Islam—as discussed in Section III: Understanding *Shirk* and Section IV: Understanding the Terminology "*Mushrik*", "People of the Book", and "Muslim".

10.   Analysis on the Concept of Muslim Men Marrying Women from the People of the Book

The following is the main verse which talks about a Muslim man marrying a woman of the People of the Book:

"This day are (all) things good and pure made lawful unto you. The food of the People of the Book is lawful unto you and yours is lawful unto them. (Lawful unto you in marriage) are (not only) chaste women who are believers but chaste women among the People of the Book revealed before your time when ye give them their due dowers and desire chastity not lewdness nor secret intrigues. If anyone rejects faith, fruitless is his work and in the Hereafter he will be in the ranks of those who have lost (all spiritual good)." (Qur'an Al-Ma'ida 5:5)

It is quite clear from this verse that the woman must be chaste for her to be considered for marriage. This is a primary condition.

In respect to understanding who the People of the Book, mentioned in this verse, there is a difference of opinion. The Question revolves around—if the statement refers to all Christians and Jew or does it refer to a sub-class of Christians and Jews. In terms of who the Muslim men can marry, there are two distinct opinions on this, and they have been discussed below:

- Islam Does Not Allow Muslim Men to Marry Women of the People of the Book.

- Islam Allows Muslim Men to Marry Women of the People of the Book.

A. Islam Does Not Allow Muslim Men to Marry Women of the People of the Book

As discussed earlier, the People of the Book are of two categories: Believers and Disbelievers. The scholars and *Ulemas* allow the Muslim man to marry the believers (who in reality are Muslims) from the People of the Book, as described earlier in Section IV: Understanding the Terminology "*Mushrik*", "People of the Book", and "Muslim". However, in respect to the Disbelievers from the People of the Book, some Scholars hold the position that Islam does not allow Muslim man to marry woman of the People of the Book, who commit *Shirk*. They based their arguments on the following summarization of Qur'anic verses and Aḥadīth.

- Christians who ascribe to the Trinity concept commits *Shirk*.

- People of the Book who take their Scholars, Rabbi, Monks as Lord Beside Allah—Who Counters Allah's Commands commits *Shirk*.

- People of the Book who take Uzair (*Alaihes-Salam*) and Jesus (*Alaihes-Salam*) as the sons of God commits

Shirk.

- People of the Book who follow Ones' Passion or *Nafs* over Allah's Commandments commits *Shirk.*

- Don't take the Jews and Christians as your friend or protector.

- Don't take your fathers and brothers as guardians if they love unbelief over belief.

- If you obey the Disbelievers and perform acts that are contrary to Islam, then you become like them and have strayed away from the Straight Path.

- Try to marry one who is religious. Certainly a Muslim woman is more religious than a Christian or Jew, who have been condemned to Hell.

- All Jews and Christians who heard about the Prophet's message and have died without believing will be in Hellfire.

- Ibn Umar considers the Christians to be *Mushrik* for believing Jesus to be the son of God, and accordingly, is strongly against Muslim Man marrying them.

- Muslims are requested not to follow the People of the Book and if they do, then they become like them and have strayed away from the Straight Path. Similarly, they are asked not to eat on the utensils of the people of the book, if other proper utensils are available.

This group of scholars, while they accept the *Ayat* of Sūrah Maidah which states that a Muslim can marry a woman from the People of the Book if they are chaste, they say that the *Ayat* is specifically applicable to Believers from the People of the Book and not to the current day People of the Book who commits Shirk. Also, they observe that this logic is similar to not eating the pig's meat or drinking alcohol when the Sūrah

Al-Ma'ida *ayat* permits eating food of the people of the Book. The separate Qur'anic *Ayat* which forbids drinking alcohol and eating meat of the pig overrides the *Ayat* which permits eating food of the People of the Book. Similarly, the Qur'anic *Ayat* on not marrying *Mushriks* which includes People of the Book as stated in various parts of the Qur'an over-rides the Qur'anic *Ayat* which permits marrying People of the Book.

The group of scholars believes that since Qur'an has repeatedly condemned *Shirk* and warned Muslim from taking friends/protectors from the People of the Book, even if they were their brothers or fathers then how one could take a woman who commits *Shirk* as one's wife. Also, when a Muslim is asked to avoid the utensils of the People of the Book, and to avoid adopting their ways, then how does one take them as a wife? The wife, being a protector/guardian of the house will have access to wealth and upbringing of the child and definitely can influence the children to follow her religion.

According to Imam Shafi'ī, as stated in his book "Al-Umm" or "The Mother" in Vol. #5 under the title "Miscellaneous chapters on marriage, divorce, etc" and under the subtitle of "Marriage of the free women of the People of the Book", a Muslim men can marry the free women of the people of the two famous books, *i.e.* the Torah and the Bible (*i.e.* the Jews and Christians) unless it is known that they disagree with the mainstream Jews and Christians in one of their major fundamentals aspects of religion as it relates to what is legal and illegal. If they do, it will be illegal to marry them just like it is illegal to marry the Magus women, who are fire worshippers. However, if the woman shares the beliefs with the mainstream Jews and Christians as far as the fundamentals of their religion is concerned but have their own way of interpreting some issues, then this does not make them illegal to get married to.

However, it is illegal, according to Imam Shafi'ī, to marry an Arab woman who currently follows Judaism or Christianity— because the original religion they had followed was Hanifiyyah (the way of Ibrahim). The Arabs went astray from the way of Ibrahim and started worshipping idols. Later they embraced Christianity. Accordingly, they are not original followers of Judaism or Christianity and hence a Muslim man cannot marry an Arab Christian or Jews.

According to Imam Shafi'ī the same rule applies to anyone whose ancestors were idol worshipers but later adopted Judaism or Christianity.

Also, Imam Shafi'ee in his book "The Mother" quotes Ataa Ibn Abi Rabaah', a prominent Tabi'i to have said the following:

> "The Arab Christians are not people of the book. The people of the book are Bani Isra'īl and those on whom Torah and Bible was sent down to (including their descendants). Those who joined them (from other people or group) are not considered from them".

B. Islam Allows Muslim Man to Marry Women of the People of the Book

The majority of the Muslim scholars and *Ulemas* are of the opinion that a Muslim man is allowed to marry a woman of the people of the Book. They based their argument on the fact that the People of the Book were already committing *Shirk* when the permission to marry them was given as evidenced by the following Qur'anic *Ayat*:

> *"O People of the Book! Commit no excesses in your religion: Nor say of Allah aught but the truth. Christ Jesus the son of Mary was (no more than) an apostle of Allah, and His Word, which He bestowed on Mary, and a spirit proceeding from Him: so believe in Allah and His*

apostles. Say not "Trinity": desist: it will be better for you: for Allah is one Allah. Glory be to Him: (far exalted is He) above having a son. To Him belong all things in the heavens and on earth. And enough is Allah as a Disposer of affairs." (Qur'an An-Nisa' 4:171)

and also, other Ayats listed earlier in Section III: Understanding Shirk. The rest of the section has been organized as follows:

- Condition Under which a Muslim men can marry a women of the People of the Book.

- Views of the Various Muslim Scholars.

- Conclusion on whether a Muslim man can marry a women from the People of the Book.

1. Condition under which a Muslim men can marry a women of the People of the Book

The Muslim scholars, however, allows such marriage under the following conditions:

- The woman from the People of the Book must be chaste as evidenced in the Qur'anic verse Al-Ma'ida 5:5, discussed above.

  Comments: Considering the current state of the women of the People of the Book in the West, it is near to impossible in identifying a girl/woman who did not have pre-marital sex. Accordingly, marriage to a person of the People of the Book becomes questionable from the very start.

- It is desirable that the woman is a resident of a Muslim country.

  Comments: If this is not the case, then the potential of the children adopting the faith of the mother is high and also the government of that country is expected to support the mother in her effort to have custody of the children. In this way a Muslim man may inadvertently facilitate his children's conversion to *Shirk*, the biggest sin in Islam. Also, a Muslim man may end up attending his Christian /Jewish wife's funeral in a church/synagogue since the wife family/relatives would not allow a Muslim funeral and accordingly, there will be no prayer / Qur'an recitation.

- The woman must be practicing her religion sincerely and she must not only be chaste but must believe in the right and wrong and uphold justice

When the above conditions are met, a Muslim man is allowed to marry a woman from the People of the Book irrespective of the fact whether the woman believes Jesus to be the son of God or believes in the concept of trinity or believes Jesus to be God. The Muslim scholars argue that the specific marriage verse mentioned above was revealed when the People of the Book were already known for committing those acts, and hence all marriage is allowed irrespective of their *Shirk* status. The *Ulemas* argue that this verse (Qur'an Al-Ma'ida 5:5) over-rides all other Qur'anic *Ayats* and Aḥadīth that have been listed and discussed earlier.

2. Views of the Various Muslim Scholars

Various views of the *Sahabas* including *Madhhabs* and contemporary scholars have been provided below:

a. View of notable Muslim *Salaf as-Salehīn*:

The fact that one is allowed to marry the People of the Book is the position held by Mujahid, Ikrimah, Said bin Jubayr, Mukhul, Al-Hasan, Ad-Dahhak, Zayd bin Aslam and Ar-Rabi bin Anas and others—May Allah be pleased with them all (Source: Tafsir Ibn Khatir who references Ibn Abi Hatim 2:669-671).

b. View of Umar bin Khattab:

Abu Jafar bin Jarir (At-Tabari) said, after mentioning that there is *Ijma* that marrying women from the People of the Scripture is allowed, "Umar disliked this practice so that the Muslims do not refrain from marrying Muslim Women, or for similar reasons (Source: Tafsir Ibn Khatir who references At-Tabari 4:366). An authentic chain of narrators stated that Shaqiq said: Once Hudhayfah married a Jewish woman and Umar wrote to him, "Divorce her". He wrote back, "Do you claim that she is not allowed for me so that I divorce her? He said, "No, but I fear that you might marry the whores from among them". Ibn Jarir related that Zayd bin Wahb said that Umar bin Khattab said, "The Muslim man marries the Christian woman, but the Christian man does not marry the Muslim woman" (Source: Tafsir Ibn Khatir who references At-Tabari 4:366).

c. View of Maulana Muhammad Yousuf Ludhianvi.

A well-known Muslim scholar from Pakistan published the following "*Fatwa*" in the Pakistani newspaper "*Jang*" answering a question regarding the shar'iah position of marriages in the US with non-Muslim women. This question was asked by a Pakistani Muslim, living in the US, and it appeared in Maulana's column that is published every Friday in a daily newspaper, "*Jang*". He interprets the Islamic law as following: "Non-Muslim women, to whom Muslim men can marry, are the women from Christian and Jewish religions who are residents of "*Daar-ul-Islam*" nations where Islamic law prevails) and who are thereby called, "*Dhi'mmi*" (those who give *Jazzia* instead of

Zakat in an Islamic state), but NOT the residents of "*Dar al-kufr*" (where the *kuffar* or non-Islamic rule exist). To these women, marriage is allowed but is "*mukrūh   tanzihi.*"   (Source: http://community.beliefnet.com/go/ thread/view/51633/13432699/muslim_woman_marr ying_People_of_the_Book?pg=3)

d. View of Abdullah Ibn `Abbas

According to Ibn 'Abbas, a Muslim may marry from among the women of the People of the Book who are the subjects of the Islamic State but is not permitted to marry from among the women of the People of the Book living in the regions which are at war with the Islamic State or are living in a territory of the unbelievers. Source: Tafsir of verse Al-Ma'ida 5:5 of Sayyid Abul Ala Maududi Tafhim al-Qur'an—The Meaning of the Qur'an in Englishtafsir.com

e. View of Sheikh Ahmed Ibn Naqib Al-Misri

In his book "*Reliance of the Traveller*" translated by Nuh Ha Mim Keller, Al-Misri observes that it is not lawful or valid for a Muslim man to be married to any woman who is not either a Muslim, Christian or Jew; nor is it lawful or valid for a Muslim woman to be married to anyone besides a Muslim Believer.

f. View of Dr. Yusuf Al-Qaradhawi

According to Yusuf Al-Qaradhawi, a contemporary Muslim scholar, marriage to Jewish and Christian women are lawful to Muslim men for they are *Ahl al-Kitab*, that is People of the Book, whose tradition is based upon the Divenly Book Torah and Injil / Bible. This position assumes that the women of the People of the Book are chaste. Dr. Al-Qaradhawi further observes in his book "*The Lawful and the Prohibited in Islam*" the following:

- It is also obvious that a Muslim woman, regardless of who she is, is better suited to a Muslim man than a woman of Christian or Jewish faith, regardless of her merits. If a Muslim man has the slightest suspicion that a non-Muslim wife might affect the beliefs and attitudes of his children, it becomes obligatory on him to exercise caution.

- If the number of Muslims in a country is small—for example, if they are immigrants residing in a non-Muslim country—their men ought to be prohibited from marrying non-Muslim women because, since Muslim women are prohibited from marrying non-Muslim men, their marriage to non-Muslim women means that many Muslim girls will remain unmarried. Since this situation is injurious to the Muslim society, this injury can be avoided by temporarily suspending this permission.

g. Views of the Hanafi *Madhab*

The Hanafis differ a little from Ibn Abbas point of view. They consider it undesirable, though not unlawful, to marry women from among the People of the Book living in a foreign territory. On the contrary, Said bin Musayyib and Hasan Basri are of the opinion that the Command is of a general nature; therefore there is no need to make any kind of distinction between the People of the Book whether they are subjects of an Islamic State or living in a foreign territory. Source: Tafsir of verse Al-Ma'ida 5:5 of Sayyid Abul Ala Maududi Tafhim al-Qur'an—The Meaning of the Qur'an in Englishtafsir.com

h.   View of Imam Shafi'ī

Imam Shafi'ī position as stated in *"Al-Umm"* or 'the "Mother" in vol. #5 under the title 'Miscellaneous chapters on marriage, divorce, *etc.*' and under the subtitle of "Marriage of the free women of the People of the Book" is as follows:

A Muslim can marry the free women of the people of the two famous books, i.e., the Torah and the Injil / Bible (*i.e.*, the Jews and Christians) unless it is known that they disagree with the mainstream Jews and Christians in one of their major fundamentals aspects of religion as it relates to what is legal and illegal. If they do, it will be illegal to marry them just like it is illegal to marry the Magus women, who are fire worshippers. However, if the woman shares the beliefs with the mainstream Jews and Christians as far as the fundamentals of their religion is concerned but have their own way of interpreting some issues, then this does not make them illegal to get married to.

However, it is illegal to marry an Arab woman who currently follows Judaism or Christianity—because the original religion they had followed was Hanifiyyah (the way of Ibrahim). The Arabs went astray from the way of Ibrahim and started worshipping idols. Later they embraced Christianity. Accordingly, they are not original followers of Judaism or Christianity and hence a Muslim man cannot marry an Arab Christian or Jew.

The same rule applies to anyone whose ancestors were idol worshipers but later adopted Judaism or Christianity.

Also, Imam Shafi'ee in his book "The Mother" quotes Ataa Ibn Abi Rabaah', a prominent Tabi'i to have said the following: "the Arab Christians are not people of the book. The people of the book are Bani Isra'īl and those on whom Torah and Bible was sent down to (including their descendants). Those who joined them (from other people or group) are not considered from them."

3. Conclusion on whether a Muslim man can marry a women from the People of the Book

The majority of the scholars are of the opinion that a Muslim man can marry a woman from the People of the Book subject to the conditions discussed earlier. However, decision on marriage is a decision normally made with the heart— and when a decision of the heart is concerned, people do not generally think rationally and overlook the primary requirement of a woman being "chaste", and accordingly are prone to making the wrong decision.

We must be careful in making *Haram* something that has been permitted specifically in the Qur'an and the Sunnah. At the same time, we must consider all the relevant verses in the Qur'an and aḥadīth as interpreted by *Ulama/fukaha* to come to the right conclusion on a specific topic. I will conclude my discussion with the Muslim ḥaīīth 3882 in Volume 3 which discusses what to do in case of a difference of opinion on a particular topic:

"Both lawful and unlawful things are evident but in between them there are matters that are not clear. So, whoever saves himself from these unclear things/matter, he saves his religion and his honor. And whoever indulges in these unclear matters, he will have fallen into the prohibitions just like a shepherd who grazes (his animals) near a private pasture, at any moment he is liable to enter it".

11. Analysis on the Concept of Muslim Women Marrying Men of the People of the Book

The Muslim Ulemas and Scholars are in 100% agreement that a Muslim woman is not allowed to marry any person from outside her faith. This includes both *Mushrik* and members of the People of the Book, who can either be Jews or Christians. The subject of Muslim woman marrying a *Mushrik* is covered in Section IX Muslim Marrying *Mushrik*. This section only deals with the subject of a Muslim woman marrying a man from the People of the Book. It has been organized as follows:

- Various Proof from the Qur'an that shows Muslim women are not allowed to marry men from the People of the Book, and.

- Views of the Scholars.

- A conclusion on whether Muslim women are allowed to marry men of the People of the Book.

A. Various Proofs from Qur'an and Sunnah that Shows Muslim Women are not Allowed to Marry Men from the People of the Book

1. Muslims are not Allowed to Marry *Mushrik*

Both Muslim men and women have been forbidden to marry Mushrik according to the Qur'anic verse Al-Baqarah 2:221:

"Do not marry unbelieving women (idolaters) until they believe; a slave woman who believes is better than an unbelieving woman even though she allure you. Nor marry (your girls) to unbelievers until they believe: a man slave who believes is better than an unbeliever even though he allure you. Unbelievers do (but) beckon you to the fire. But Allah beckons by His grace to the Garden (of Bliss) and forgiveness and makes His Signs clear to mankind: that they may celebrate His praise".

Earlier in Section III and Section IV, we observed from the various Qur'anic *Ayats* and Aḥadīth that Jews and Christians commit *Shirk*. We noted that the Christians have *Mushrik* values —they believe in Trinity; believe in Jesus as the son of God; and believing Jesus to be God himself. We also observed that the Unitarians who claim to believe in the Oneness's of God also commit *Shirk* as they believe Jesus to be the son of God and also because they follow their *Nafs* in defining the structure and fundamentals of their religion. The Unitarians do not follow either the Torah or the Bible but define and follow their own rules of worship.

Similarly, we learnt that the Jews commit *Shirk* by claiming Uzair (*Alehe-ssalam*) as the son of God and by taking their Scholars and Rabbi's as Lord beside Allah when they are changing or adding new God's commandments—basically giving in to their *Nafs*.

In Tafsir Ibn Kathir Volime 1, the author observes that in the above Verse Al-Baqarah 2:221,

> *"The meaning is general and includes every Mushrik woman from among the idol worshippers and the People of the Scriptures"*.

In the same Tafsir Book of Volume 3, page 104, Ibn Abi Hatim recorded that Abu Malik Al-Ghifari said that Ibn Abbas said that when this Ayat was revealed, the people did not marry the pagan women. When the verse Al-Ma'ida 5:5 *"lawful to you in marriage are chase women from the People of the believers and chaste women from the People of the Scriptures before your time"*, was revealed, they married women from the People of the Book.

In Bukhari Ḥadīth 209, Volume 7 and narrated by Nafi:

> "Whenever Ibn 'Umar was asked about marrying a Christian lady or a Jewess, he would say: "Allah has made it unlawful for the believers to marry ladies who ascribe partners in worship to Allah, and I do not know of a greater thing, as regards to ascribing partners in worship, *etc.* to Allah, than that a lady should say that Jesus is her Lord although he is just one of Allah's slaves."

Accordingly, a Muslim woman is not allowed to marry a man of the People of the Book because he is a *Mushrik*.

2. The Verse which Permits Marrying from the People of the Book is Restricted to Men only

The verse "This day are (all) things good and pure made lawful unto you. The food of the People of the Book is lawful unto you and yours is lawful unto them. (Lawful unto you in marriage) are (not only) chaste women who are believers but chaste women among the People of the Book revealed before your time when ye give them their due dowers and desire chastity not lewdness nor secret intrigues. If anyone rejects faith, fruitless is his work and in the Hereafter he will be in the ranks of those who have lost (all spiritual good)". (Qur'an Al-Ma;ida 5:5)

We learnt in Verse al-Baqarah 2:221 above that Muslims (both men and women) were forbidden to marry *Mushriks*, which includes People of the Book. However, Allah provided an exception in verse Al-Ma;ida 5:5 above for the Muslim man to marry a woman from the People of the Book. **The Qur'an, however, does not grant the same exception for a Muslim woman to marry a man of the People of the Book.**

Accordingly, a Muslim woman is not allowed to marry a man of the People of the Book because he is a Mushrik.

3.   Muslim Women are only Allowed to Marry Believers

The Qur'anic *Ayat* An-Nur 24:3 states

> *"The fornicator does not marry except a fornicatress (female) or an idolatress, and the fornicatress shall not marry anyone but a fornicator or an idolator and that (marrying them) is haram for the believers"*

Based on the above Qur'anic *Ayat*, a believer, either men or women, is forbidden to marry a fornicator. This includes marrying a Muslim fornicator unless he or she repents. A fornicator is not in Islam when he/she is committing an act of adultery according to Bukhari Ḥadīth 484 in Volume 7 as narrated by Abu Huraira:

> "The Prophet ﷺ said, "An adulterer, at the time he is committing illegal sexual intercourse is not a believer; and a person, at the time of drinking an alcoholic drink is not a believer; and a thief, at the time of stealing, is not a believer."

Ibn Shihab said: 'Abdul Malik bin Abi Bakr bin 'Abdur-Rahman bin Al- Harith bin Hisham told me that Abu Bakr used to narrate that narration to him on the authority of Abu Huraira. He used to add that Abu Bakr used to mention, besides the above cases,

"And he who robs (takes illegally something by force) while the people are looking at him, is not a believer at the time he is robbing (taking) it".

Comment: In Tafsir of verse An-Nur 24:3, Sayyid Abul Ala Maududi in his Tafhim al-Qur'an—The Meaning of the Qur'an as documented in Englishtafsir.com notes the following:

Only an adulterous woman is a fit match for an adulterous man who has not repented, or for such a man an idolatrous woman. No believing, virtuous woman can be a match for an adulterous man. It is forbidden for the Believers that they should give their daughters in marriage to such wicked people knowing them to be so. Similarly, the tit match for adulterous women (who have not repented) can only be adulterous or idolatrous men; they are not fit for any righteous Believer. It is forbidden for the Believers that they should marry women who are known to possess immoral character. This thing applies to those men and women who persist in their evil ways, and not to those who repent and reform themselves, for after repentance and reformation they will no longer be regarded as "adulterous."

Accordingly, it can be inferred from this Qur'anic *Ayat* and the Ḥadīth mentioned above that the Muslim woman can only marry a believing Muslim man and that she cannot marry a man from the People of the Book. The same would have held true for a Muslim man also if not for the Qur'anic verse 5:5, which provides an exception for the Muslim man to marry a woman from the People of the Book.

4. Fourth Proof: Muslim Women are only Allowed to Marry Believers

The Qur'anic Verse: *"O ye who believe! When there come to you believing women refugees, examine (and test) them: Allah knows best as to their Faith: if ye ascertain that they are Believers, then send them not back to the Unbelievers (Kafirs). They are not lawful (wives) for the Unbelievers, nor are the (Unbelievers) lawful (husbands) for them. But pay the Unbelievers what they have spent (on their dower), and there will be no blame on you if ye marry them on payment of their dower to them. But hold not to the guardianship of unbelieving women: ask for what ye have spent on their dowers, and let the (Unbelievers) ask for what they have spent (on the dowers of women who come over to you). Such is the command of Allah: He judges (with justice) between you. And Allah is Full of Knowledge and Wisdom".* (Qur'an Al-Mumtahina 60:10)

Comments: Imam Ash Shawkani in his *tafsir* book "*Fathul Qadīr*" states that this verse is a strong proof (*Dalīl*) which prohibits believing woman marrying a disbelieving man. Imam Qurtubi also states that this verse is the biggest *Dalīl* which prohibits believing woman marrying a disbelieving man.

In Tafsir of verse Al-Mumtahina 60:10, Sayyid Abul Ala Maududi in his Tafhim al-Qur'an—The Meaning of the Qur'an as documented in Englishtafsir.com notes the following:

And if Islam has been accepted by the woman and the man remains an infidel—whether he is a follower of an earlier scripture or a non-follower, the Hanafi Madhab say that Islam will be presented before the husband whether consummation between them has taken place or not. If he accepts it, the woman will continue to be his wife; if he rejects it the *qadi* will affect separation between them. So long as the man does not refuse to accept Islam, the woman will remain his wife, but he will not have the right to have sexual relations with her. In case the husband refuses, separation will become effective just like an irrevocable divorce. If consummation has not taken place before this, the woman will be entitled to half the dower, and if it has taken place, the woman will be entitled to full dower as well as maintenance during the waiting period (*iddat*). (Al-Mabsut; Hedayah; Fath at-Qadir). According to Imam Shafe`i, marriage will dissolve as soon as the woman accepted Islam in case consummation has not taken place, and in case it has taken place, the woman will continue to be the man's wife till the end of the waiting period. If in the meantime he accepts Islam, marriage will remain valid, otherwise separation will take place as soon as the waiting period comes to an end.

Summary of the Various Proofs:

The first and second proofs essentially eliminate the permissibility of a Muslim woman marrying a man of the People of the Book who commits *Shirk*. The Third and Fourth proofs forbid a Muslim woman marrying a disbeliever (*Kafir*). So based on all the four proofs, a Muslim woman is forbidden, according to Muslim scholars, to marry a man of the People of the Book whether he commits *Shirk* or is a Disbeliever (*Kafir*)

B. Various Views of the Scholars

There is a unanimous agreement among the Muslim Scholars about the impermissibility of a Muslim woman marrying a man from the People of the Book. The Islamic position on few of the scholars and organizations have been provided below:

1. Sheikh Yusuf Al-Qaradawi

    It is *haram* for a Muslim woman to marry a non-Muslim man, regardless of whether he is of the People of the Book or not. We have already mentioned the saying of Allah,

    "... and do not marry (your girls) to idolaters until they believe ..." (Qur'an Al-Baqarah 2: 221)

    And He said concerning the immigrant Muslim women:

    "Then if you know them to be Believers, do not send them back to the unbelievers. They are not lawful for them (as wives), nor are they lawful for them (as husbands)." (Qur'an Al-Mumtahina 60: 10)

    No text exists which makes exceptions for the People of the Book. Hence, on the basis of the above verses, there is a consensus among Muslims concerning this prohibition. (Source: The Lawful and the Prohibited in Islam)

2. Sheikh Ahmed Ibn Naqib Al-Misri

    In his book "*Reliance of the Traveller*" translated by Nuh Ha Mim Keller, Al-Misri observes that it is not lawful or valid for a Muslim man to be married to any woman who is not either a Muslim, Christian or Jew; **nor is it lawful or valid for a Muslim woman to be married to anyone besides a Believer.**

3. Sayyid Sabiq

    "The scholars are unanimous that it is not permissible for a Muslim woman to marry a non-Muslim, whether he is a pagan or from People of the Book." (Sabiq, Sayyid, *Fiqh as-Sunnah*, Vol.2, 105 -) http://thedefiance.co/marriage_ with_ disbelievers

4. Kuwaiti Encyclopedia of Jurisprudence

   Likewise, it is stated in *al-Mawsuat al-Fiqhiya al-Kuwaitiya* (Kuwaiti Encyclopedia of Jurisprudence):

   "A Muslim woman's marriage with a non-Muslim is not permissible, whether he is a *dhimmi* or one from People of the Book. This is by the agreement of the jurists."

   (*al-Mawsuat al-Fiqhiya al-Kuwaitiya*, Vol.7, 133)
   http://thedefiance.co/marriage_with_disbelievers

5. Companions' View on Verse 2:221 (Source: http://thedefiance .co/marriage_with_disbelievers)

   The Prophet's Companions (*Sahabas*) and most of the scholars of later generations have understood the word "*mushrikat*" in Qur'an Al-Baqarah 2:221 to refer to Jewish/Christian women as well. 'Abdullah bin 'Umar did not approve marriage with Christian women. He used to say:

   "I do not know shirk greater than a person saying "Isa (Alaihes-Salam) is his Lord" and Allah has said, "*And do not marry polytheistic women until they believe*"." (Qur'an Al-Baqarah 2:221).

   Ibn 'Abbas said: When the verse

   "'And do not marry polytheistic women until they believe' was revealed people stayed away from [all] polytheistic (mushrik) women until subsequent revelation of the verse, 'And [lawful to you in marriage] are chaste women of the people who were given the Book before you'." (Qur'an Al-Ma'ida 5:5)

Thereafter, the people married women of People of the Book. (Ibn Kathir, *Tafisr al-Qur'an al-'Azim*, Vol.3, 38)

Ibn al-Jawzi (d. 597/1200) writes

> "On the word "*mushrikat*" there are two opinions: One is to take it in general sense including women of People of the Book and others. This is the opinion of the majority. And second is that it is specific to pagan women, and this is the saying of Sa'id bin Jubayr, al-Nakha'i and Qatadah."

> [Ibn al-Jawzi, *Zaad al-Maysar*, Vol.1, 188]

Narrations with al-Tabari and Ibn Abi Hatim tell us that among the majority who counted Jews and Christians as polytheists (*mushrikin*) include companions like Ibn 'Abbas (*ra*) and Ibn 'Umar (*ra*).

It must, however, be remembered that even the few odd early scholars and those who followed them in saying that the verse is specific to pagan women never ruled the permissibility of a Muslim woman's marriage to a non-Muslim man. Apparently, they said so only in wake of Qur'an 5:5 which effectively limits the Qur'an Al-Baqarah 2:221 to pagan women. Whereas the majority commented to the verse in its own right even though they also knew that in the final assessment the prohibition for Muslim men is only regarding pagan women.

It should be noted that despite their mutual difference both Ibn 'Umar (*ra*) and Ibn 'Abbas (*ra*) considered "*mushrikat*" (polytheist women) to include Jewish/Christian women as well. And if "*mushrikat*" in Al-Baqarah 2:221 includes Jewish/Christian women, naturally "*mushrikin*" (polytheist men) in the same verse includes Jewish/Christian men as well. And then we have exception for Jewish/Christian women (where Muslim men are allowed to marry Jewish/Christian women) but nothing of the kind for Jewish/Christian men (where Muslim women were allowed to marry Jewish/Christian men).

C. Conclusion on Whether Muslim Women are Allowed to Marry Men of the People of the Book

While articles have been written by progressive individual or western media about the permissibility of Muslim women marrying men of the People of the Book, **the Islamic perspective on this subject is very clear.** *i.e.,* **Muslim women are not allowed to marry men of the People of the Book.** This position is based on the Qur'an verses and views of the *Sahabas* and scholars mentioned above.

May Allah forgive me if I have presented anything incorrectly and guide me and you to the right decision.